The Flying Artist's Guide to Sketching

SpiceBox

More than creative packaging

Published by Spicebox 2006
3918 Kitchener Street, Burnaby, BC,
Canada

Printed in China.

Photography by Peter Raymond, Southport.
Origination by DL Repro Ltd., London EC
1 M 4DD.
Book design by JW Veldhoen

ISBN 1-894426-53-3

Contents

About the Author
Philip Berrill The Flying Artist

Philip Berrill is a professional artist, tutor, lecturer, and author—his method of learning to paint taught and enjoyed worldwide. Born in 1945 in Northampton, England, Philip now lives in Southport with his wife Sylvia, and daughter Penelope.

Philip recalls how he discovered paint at age three. It was a sunny afternoon, he wandered into his father's greenhouse and saw at the far end of the building a large bucket of whitewash, and a tubular pump sprayer. Philip loaded the sprayer, and had a lovely afternoon covering all of his father's best tomatoes and plants with white. He had discovered paint, and that it could change how you see the world.

Author, artist, lecturer, Philip Berrill

At the age of fourteen, Philip decided he would make a living as a professional artist. He came under the influence of the Welsh artist and tutor John Sullivan. Philip held his first solo exhibition at the age of eighteen, followed by other group, and solo exhibitions. At the age of twenty-eight, Liverpool University held a major exhibition of his work — the direct result of which was that Philip could realize his ambition to become a professional artist. He launched very successful art classes using his unique approach to teaching, sketching, and painting. These classes proved so popular Philip went on to develop worldwide correspondence courses. In the 1980s, he embarked on the next stage of his career that led to his being nicknamed The Flying Artist. After offering sought-after painting vacation courses in Great Britain, he

organized additional painting holiday retreats in Europe — in Rome, Venice, Florence, and Paris. Subsequently Philip lectured and demonstrated painting in America and the Middle East. Philip's much-admired exhibition, The Italian Connection, consists of sketches and paintings from his Italian journeys, and other European locations. Philip's love and enthusiasm for sketching and painting is infectious. He believes that art should be for everyone, and that you are never too young, or too old, to begin sketching. His students have ranged from ten to eighty, and he continues to enjoy passing on his enthusiasm and knowledge, gained over thirty years, to people from all walks of life. Philip has designed his method for people of all ages and all abilities, and over recent years has produced a series of art videos.

These videos led to an invitation to produce and present a thirteen-part television series *Paint with the Flying Artist* and that project in turn led to the writing and illustration of this series of art books designed especially for you — books meant to cover a wide range of mediums, techniques, and subjects introducing you to the joy and pleasure of sketching and painting. These beautifully presented books come with all the materials you will need to get started painting and drawing. The compact form and portability of the kit allows freedom and spontaneity to capture each moment of inspiration that Philip demonstrates in his own work. The hope is that these kits will assist you in your journey of sketching and painting.

Philip was painting one day in Venice. A film crew appeared and started to record a television commercial close by. The model, the car, and the wonderful Venetian backdrop presented a new subject. Philip broke off from the scene that he was painting, and quickly sketched this unique subject.

Introduction

"A B S", means Always Be Sketching, and is a favorite saying of mine. If you have ever said, "I wish I could paint, but I can't draw a straight line", then sketching could be the first step to introducing you to the marvelous world of art.

Why Sketch?

Not only can sketching be fun in its own right, it is also key to creating successful paintings. Experience has taught me that many people who already paint greatly underestimate the value of sketching, when in fact it is the most economical introduction to learning the essentials of picture making. Many of the old masters were great sketchers and if they found sketching important and worthwhile, we should treat sketching with equally seriousness. Whether a newcomer to painting, or at a more advanced stage, I invite you to join me, read and sketch your way through this book, and discover the delights sketching can offer you.

What is a Sketch?

It is important to spend a few moments thinking about exactly what a sketch is. What does it set out to achieve? How much information is included in a sketch? Can you sketch in different mediums? Is a sketch black and white only, or can you sketch in color? What is the difference between sketching and drawing? A sketch is a versatile way to express ideas, and to put down on paper the initial visual information about a subject. The subject can be real, from a photograph, inspired by poetry, prose, music, or from your imagination.

Philip Berrill at work in plein air.

A sketch is often the first exploratory stage for a painting, a part of the preparation for a finished work. Sketches should be flexible — they should alter, change, and adapt. Sometimes a sketch is just a few fleeting lines that capture the essentials of the subject. At other times, a sketch may contain more information, including details on light and shade, textures and color notes. When you do not have time to paint a picture you can make a quick sketch and take a photograph of it. The sketch and photograph will allow you to paint a picture of the view at home or in your studio.

You can use anything that makes a mark to sketch. The great joy of sketching is that you can start with a humble pencil on the back of an envelope — you do not need fancy equipment or expensive paper. Many sketches have spontaneity and freshness that can be difficult to capture in a finished painting. This is often because when painting, people try too hard to get the painting just right, whereas one is more relaxed when sketching, and less worried about making mistakes. This spontaneity in painting comes from speed, the speed comes from experience, and that experience comes from practice. Sketching is practice.

Don't confuse sketching with drawing, sketches contain as little or as much information as you feel is necessary. An artist determines the subject, content, composition, and style of a drawing. A sketch tends to be looser, more exploratory, and sometimes incomplete. However, many sketches will stand as attractive, viable, and saleable artworks in their own right. Sketching is essentially the visual expression of ideas about real or imaginary subjects.

A selection of sketches from Philip Berrill's portfolio

Materials For Sketching

Early cave painters of France and Spain produced the most dramatic images with very basic materials — there were no art shops to buy supplies, so they had to improvise. There were no art teachers to help them, yet they produced stunning pictures based on their own experiences, communicating their images and thoughts. We are fortunate to have a superb selection of art materials conveniently available from art shops at affordable prices. The materials we buy and use today developed from the knowledge, skills, experience, and needs of artists, and from their desire to create images over the centuries.

All you need to start sketching is a pencil and a sheet of paper. If you look around your home, you will be able to find many other suitable materials for sketching, including ballpoint pens, pencils, fountain pens, felt-tipped and nylon-tipped pens, colored pens and plain copy paper or writing paper. It is possible to sketch in a wide range of other mediums including colored pencils, watercolors, pastels, and oil paints. We will look at these techniques using color in later stages in this book.

Pencils

Pencils are a mixture of graphite and china clay. The more graphite there is in the pencil, the softer it is, and the darker the mark that it will make. The more china clay in the mixture, the harder the pencil, and the sharper mark it will make. The pencil lead mounts in wood, and is circular or hexagonal in shape. Soft pencils are B, harder pencils H. They also come numbered two through nine — the higher the number the softer, or harder, the pencil. 2B and 3B are medium soft and ideal for sketching. 7, 8 and 9B are too soft and smudgy for general work, but do have their uses. The H pencils are too hard for most artwork, and preferred for technical or engineering drawing. HB pencils are in everyday use for writing as an all-purpose pencil.

Carpenters' Pencils

Made in a similar manner to the traditional round pencils, but rectangular, carpenter's pencils sharpen to a chisel-like end, and offer a different variety of pencil marks when compared to a normal pencil.

Graphite Sticks

These are sticks of graphite not bound in a wooden casing but varnished or wrapped in paper to stop the graphite from dirtying your fingers. The main advantage to using a graphite stick is that you can use the tip as a normal pencil, and the wide side of the sharp end for bold sweeps of pencil marks, and for the shading of large areas. Both carpenters' pencils and graphite sticks come in varying degrees of softness.

Materials For Sketching

Pens

Dip-in, sketching, or mapping pens are the most common. These have a metallic nib in a wooden or plastic holder. The pen is dips into ink to load the nib of the pen.

India and Colored Inks

India ink is black and lightfast meaning it (won't fade). It comes in waterproof and non-waterproof forms, but I recommend the waterproof version for sketching. Colored inks are also available, but the main problem with them is that when exposed to normal daylight for any length of time they often fade. They are ideally suited to work that will not be exposed to a great deal of light.

Fountain Pens

You can sketch with a regular fountain pen. Some manufacturers have make a range of fountain pens for sketching on the market. These use non-waterproof ink cartridges, not India ink. India ink contains a mild glue, and can clog a fountain pen, so be sure to use regular fountain pen ink. Use India ink only for dip-in pens, or brush drawing work.

Ballpoint Pens

Many find a common ballpoint pen ideal for quick sketching.

Felt-tip and Nylon-Tip Pens

The tremendous number, range of sizes and types of points on modern felt and synthetic-tip pens provide a bewildering choice for the artist. Experiment — find one or two pens you feel find comfortable with. Some pens are waterproof while, others are not. Most of the colored pens will fade in strong light. Ask your local art or stationery store to explain the qualities of the various pens they stock. Many have sample pens you can try out in the store.

Colored Pencils

Some colored pencils are water soluble, often known as aquarelle, while others are not water soluble and are used just for and work only for applying dry color. Conté Use Aquarelle pencils can be used dry, or brushed over with a wash of water to create color-life effects. A set of aquarelle pencils provides a variety of ways of using color in sketches.

Conté Carres: Crayons

These are square sticks of firm pastel. The most common colors are black, gray, white, sanguine, and sepia. They offer beautiful results, especially on tinted paper.

Sepia, Sanguine and White Conté Pastel Pencils

Similar to the crayons that I mentioned above, but in pencil format. These pencils offer exciting sketching opportunities on tinted paper.

Materials For Sketching

Carbon Graphic Pencil

Pencils designed for finer, more defined lines, and ideal for sketching and technical drawing.

Pierre Noire

Made from a filtered paste pigment, this pencil gives a deep, solid and indelible matte black.

Charcoal

Black, burnt wood. Usually made from willow wood and available in single sticks or boxed in thin, medium, thick, or assorted sticks. Charcoal can reduce to powder, remix, and reform into compressed sticks of charcoal in different pencil-like degrees of softness.

Erasers

A general, all purpose eraser is sufficient, but the one preferred by most artists is the malleable rubber eraser because it can by molded with your fingers into all sorts of shapes for rubbing out, modifying and lifting out passages or work. , It does not create loose pieces of paper and eraser so the work does not have to be dust off by hand, which in turns reduces the risk of smudging.

Fixative

Pencils, charcoal and pastels need "fixing" to prevent them from smudging.

Paper

You can get cartridge paper by the sheet, or in a pad that can be coil bound or gummed. Popular sizes are 4" x 6" (100 mm x 150mm), 6" x 8" (150mm x 200mm), 9" x 12" (230mm x 305mm), 12" x 18" (305mm x 455mm), 14" x 17" (355mm x 430mm) and 18" x 24" (455mm x 610mm). Sketching paper comes in different weights and thicknesses as well, but 80lb (110g) paper is ideal for most sketching.

Brushes

Round and flat, sable, or modern synthetic hair brushes enable color to be used either directly, or in conjunction with another sketching medium.

Pencil Sharpeners, Craft Knives, and Sandpaper

You can use any of the above tools to bring your pencil point to the shape you would like to use for the sketch you plan to make.

Paints

A pocket set of artist quality, or watercolor ½ pans provide a compact set of paints for indoor and outdoor sketching.

Materials For Sketching

Drawing Boards

You can use a clipboard for smaller sketches, or a sturdy piece of cardboard for your larger work. Custom drawing boards are often available as well.

Drawing Pins, Drawing Board Clips, Masking Tape

Try not to use drawing pins as they make marks in the board that can show through in other work if shaded or drawn over. Drawing board clips will hold the paper to the board, but I usually secure my paper with masking tape.

Tissues

Soft tissues are handy for wiping your pen nib or brush when sketching or painting.

Easels

An easel is not essential for sketching, however table easels are readily available, and many people enjoy working on them. Metal or wooden sketching easels can be very useful indoors, but are especially useful on outdoor sketching trips.

Portfolio

A 9"x 12" or 12" x 18" portfolio will keep your sketches clean and flat.

Everything you need to sketch par exellence

Sketching: Discover Your Style

There are almost as many styles of sketching as there are artists. Styles of handwriting differs as do styles of sketching. My own style is neat and tidy, but I have seen and enjoyed looking at vigorous free flowing work by other artists. Look at pictures in art galleries and museums, art publications and magazines, and look at fine art prints to discover the varied styles artists use. One artist may use a few quick lines to encapsulate the subject, another may use many lines — one artist may use little or no color, another could use vibrant colors in his or her interpretation of the same subject. You may be attracted by the style of one artist, and not another, but think how boring it would be if all sketches and paintings looked the same! Explore your own natural style by trying subjects in different sketching mediums. For the tree, I used a 2B pencil for the pencil sketch, and then I tried a monochrome sketch using a water-soluble, felt-tip pen, and created a monochrome by brushing over it with a little water. Finally, I made a pen and wash sketch in color.

The shape of the point of your pencil can make its own distinctive contribution to your sketch. While you can just pick up a pencil and sketch away, let's think about the pencil point. Do you want a sharp point giving a fine, sharp line or a more rounded point giving a different width of line? Would a duller point be beneficial to a particular sketch? The way you sharpen your pencil can make quite a difference to a sketch.

A pencil sharpener will give a clear, sharp point to the pencil. But, by using a craft knife, or pen-knife, you can vary the length of pencil lead exposed. Use the knife to slice away the wood around the pencil point. Do not try to shape the pencil lead with the knife. Always keep fingers behind cutting edges.

By rubbing the pencil point on a sheet of fine sandpaper, you can make the tip more rounded, or create a chisel-like edge to the pencil tip. Try creating sharp, pointed, rounded and chisel ends to your pencil and compare the types of lines created.

The best practice for sharpening.

Sketching: Discover Your Style

A pencil sketch

A water soluble felt brushed with water

Pen and wash

Holding Your Pencil, Pen or Brush

When first holding a pencil for drawing most people adopt the writing position (fig. 1). They rest their hand on the paper and hold the pencil in their fingers. This gives a small controlled area and allows for sketching lines and curves of a short length. This is fine for writing, but is not practical for sketching and painting.

By lifting the hand off the page, you can work from your wrist as well as your fingers (fig. 2). A single line or curve drawn from the wrist can be two to three times longer than a line drawn from the fingers when the hand is resting on the table.

Sit back in your chair with your hand still off the page. Try drawing a line from your elbow joint (fig. 3). This will give you more freedom to draw longer, free flowing lines. You will have a much larger area for your hand and arm to sweep curved and straight lines.

Finally, with your sketchpad on an easel or a tabletop, stand up and draw a line using your entire arm and shoulder (fig. 4). This will give you the largest possible area for your arm and hand to sweep and work within.

Try sketching lines on your sketchpad in the ways described above, working from your fingers, wrist, elbow, and shoulder.

fig 2. wrist

fig 3. elbow

fig 4. shoulder

fig. 1 fingers

Basic Shapes

By taking things gradually and building on sound foundations you will soon find that you can begin to sketch successfully. Rather than sketching your subject from the top and working downwards, I recommend a slightly different approach. Everything you ever draw or paint will be based on one or more basic shapes; circles, ovals, squares, rectangles, triangles and cylinders. For an apple, lightly draw a simple circle, and sketch the distinctive apple shape over that. For a coffee mug, draw a light vertical cylinder and sketch your mug on that.

A combination of basic shapes makes the sketching of a traditional telephone quite an easy task. Draw a simple triangle— add a circle for a dial, two ovals, and a curve for the handset and a long rectangle for the base.

Lightly drawing the basic shape, or shapes, of your subject will ensure it is going to sit in the right place on your sketchpad, and be of the right proportions. The subject should sit neither too high nor too low on the page, nor be too wide, too thin, too tall, nor too short.

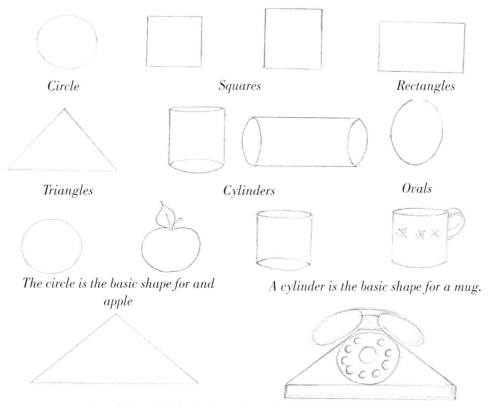

Circle *Squares* *Rectangles*

Triangles *Cylinders* *Ovals*

The circle is the basic shape for and apple

A cylinder is the basic shape for a mug.

A traditional dial telephone is made of several basic shapes: a triangle, a long rectangle, circles, ovals, and a curve for the headset

Basic Shapes

Look around your home for objects based on basic shapes. Circles, squares, rectangles, cylinders, ovals and triangles. Sketch the basic shapes and then build the objects on them.

Pencil Shading

Pencils vary in degree of softness (B) and hardness (H). Copy the chart on the right into your sketch book. H pencils to the left and B pencils to the right. Your kit comes with nine pencils, each of which has a different number and letter on the end. Find your 2B pencil, and go to No. 2 under letter B and shade a dark to light column down the page. Vary the strength of shading by varying the pressure of your hand on the pencil. As you complete the chart using your remaining pencils you will see and feel the difference in their effects.

Next take your 2B pencil to make the tone chart shown on the left below. This will help you get a feeling for the pressure you need to apply in order to achieve different tones; or degrees of light and dark with your pencil. Experiment with the other pencils to see if you can create the same effects. Soft pencil shading can be gently blended by rubbing with your fingertip for softer shading effects. In the bottom right panel I show how highlights can be "lifted out" with a kneaded eraser avoiding ragged-edged highlights.

Pencil depth chart.

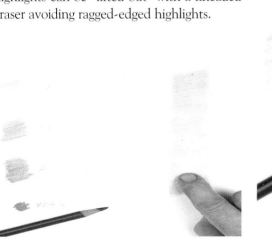

Pencil tonal strengths and blending technique.

Lifting out highlights with a kneaded eraser.

14

Monochrome Coffee Jug

The sketches on this page are worth copying into your sketch book as they will help you remember the important aspects of shading. Decide which way the source of light is coming from; the left, the right, or from above the subject. This will determine which way the shadow will fall (see diagram below). Here it is from the left, so the shadow is on the right of the jug. I show light shading, then medium and then dark on the right side of the jug. I emphasized the darkest features and picked out the highlights.

The ball and box show the two parts of shadow: the shadow on the object itself, as well as the shadow it casts onto the ground. Note the box casts two shadows, one inside and one outside. The shadow is darkest at the base of the object and becomes lighter as it travels away. Refer to the diagram below to see how the placement of a light source in your sketch affects how shadows cast.

A jug

The shadows objects cast

The higher the source of light the shorter the shadow.

Always decide where the light source is coming from to light your subject, above, the left, the right, behind or in front.

Light from the right,

Light from the left.

The lower the source of light, the longer the shadows.

The stronger the light, the darker the shadow. The softer the light, the gentler the shadow.

Hatching and Crosshatching

So far we have looked at what I call traditional pencil shading where you achieve varying tones by altering the pressure on your pencil. There is another technique in which you can use a variety of pencil lines to create other kinds of shading. They come under four headings.

Hatching is the use of parallel lines. The closer together the pencil lines, the darker the area; the further apart, the lighter the area.

Crosshatching is where one set of hatching lines is placed over another set.

Stippling is where dots are made with the pencil. The closer the dots, the darker the area; the further apart, the lighter the area.

Random lines are pencil marks, semicircles, ticks and wiggly pencil effects that do not fall under the other three headings, but can be very useful.

Draw the chart below in your sketch book. Invent several more types of hatching, crosshatching and random lines of your own. The tree to the right shows how versatile this technique can be.

Hatching

Stippling

Crosshatching

Random lines

Tactile Values

A painting consists of three main parts: the sketch or drawing of the subject, the coloring in of it and the ability to show, or suggest, the material the subject is made from.

When you look at paintings by the great masters such as Rembrandt, Gainsborough or Renoir, you do not have to guess what material they were painting in any part of their picture. Artists try to trick the eyes of onlookers into believing that a few marks of a pencil on paper is actually wood, silk, metal, hair, flesh, or whatever they may sketch. In fact, if you think of yourself as an illusionist you will be very close to understanding what much of sketching and painting is about.

We can use the traditional shading, hatching, crosshatching, stippling and random lines to gain an insight into the art of rendering textures, often referred to as tactile values. I would like you to find and sketch two very different pieces of wood, one a piece of rough tree bark, the other a smoother piece. I show these types of wood below. With one I have used hatching and crosshatching to help convey the coarse, rough surface, and with the other I have used a softer, blended shading for the smoother effect. When you have tried this exercise, look around your home for a selection of subjects with a variety of different textures. A rubber glove, a broken brick, a milk bottle or a child's furry toy are excellent examples.

See if you can capture the textural effects of the subjects. When you show the resulting sketches to your friends or family, ask them what types of material they think the items are made of. If you are given the correct answer, well done. If they give a wrong answer, look at the surface of the object again, and see if there is any more textural information that you can add to your sketch. It is well worth trying two or three sketches each month of different textured items in order to continue to develop your skill in capturing textural effects.

Rough tree bark
using hatching and crosshatching to
convey a coarse, rough surface.

For the smoother tree bark, I have used a
smoother blended shading, gently rubbing
the shading with my fingertip.

Tactile Values

Still Life

Failing to plan is planning to fail. This is sound advice which applies to almost everything in life, and certainly to sketching and painting. Always choose subjects that you feel moved or inspired by. Never just paint a subject for the sake of doing it. It is always more enjoyable to paint inspirational subjects, and this is often reflected in the quality of the work. Once you have chosen a subject, a little thought and planning goes a long way in helping ensure that you finish with a successful painting. Sketching plays a very important part in the picture planning stage. In the later stages of this book we look at picture composition, but I consider the making of preliminary sketches so important that I think this aspect should be considered at this stage. I will now take a still life subject and a lansdcape to illustrate the uses and advantages of making preliminary sketches.

Preliminary Sketch 1

I set up a simple still life subject on a table. I used a mixing bowl, two eggs, a wooden spoon, a jug and a bag of flour. I wanted to be sure of the correct positions and proportions of the items in the still life in relation to the picture area on my sketch pad. *Preliminary Sketch 1* gave me this opportunity.

Preliminary Sketch 2

Here I looked for and added more detail to the shape of the objects to give them a more definite form.

Preliminary Sketch 3

In the third, far more completed sketch on the opposing page, I decided on the direction and strength of the light, I located the light, medium and dark tones, I identified the darkest features and highlights, and finally I positioned the shadows. These three quick sketches helped me get to know the subject and identify and resolve any problem areas. At this stage I knew if I went ahead and used these preliminary sketches as the basis for a painting, I would have sound foundation.

Preliminary Sketch 1

Preliminary Sketch 2

Still Life

Preliminary Sketch 3

Landscape

With the landscape subject I used exactly the same sequence of steps as before, working from a simple preliminary sketch, below, to a more defined, light, outline sketch, shown top right on the page opposite, through to the shaded in, more defined sketch, below it. This approach may sound elementary to readers who are at an advanced stage in their painting, but it is a method I have used for over thirty years and it has never let me down. It is an excellent technique for people who are at the start of their sketching and painting activities and well worth more experienced painters trying out. Often the most successful of my students and course members are those who have adopted this approach. They find their paintings are based on a more sound foundation than those who do not use it.

People often choose the first view of a subject they see, only to find that when they stop, stand up, and move from one side to another they find a more interesting or unusual view that they wish they had worked from. If working from life, especially outdoors, it is well worth making several very quick sketches of your subject from different angles to discover the best angle for the subject, even though you may end up coming back to work from the first view or angle you saw.

Most of the mistakes in a painting are made before picking-up a paintbrush. People are so keen to get on with the painting they quickly sketch out the picture, spend many hours painting on that sketch, only to find at the end that mistakes in the sketch have been painted into the picture.

When you have made your sketch, before you shade it or paint it stop, turn the sketch upside down, or turn it to face a mirror and look at it in the mirror. Any mistake will show up and can be corrected. The corrections can be rechecked using the same methods.

Preliminary Sketch 1

Landscape

Preliminary Sketch 2

Preliminary Sketch 3

Pen and Ink Sketching

We have looked at the use of a pencil for sketching, but there are many other items and materials which can be used by artists to create an extensive range of sketching techniques and to allow for the widest varieties of style and expression. Let us look at the use of pen and ink. Pen and ink sketching is traditionally created using a bottle of black waterproof India ink and a dip-in pen. Most art shops and stationery stores keep mapping pens, or pen holders with separate pen nibs. While nylon and felt-tip pens, technical drawing pens, and fountain pens can be used, so can sharpened matchsticks, toothpicks and sharpened bamboo.

Pen and Ink Technique

Keep a spare piece of paper on the table by your side, so that as you dip into the bottle of ink you can test the pen stroke on the paper. This will ensure that there is not too much ink on the nib and that it won't blot. You may get one or two blots at first, but you soon get to know just how much ink to have on your pen. Keep a tissue in your non-painting hand so that every five minutes or so you can wipe your nib on it to stop the ink drying and clogging. The types of drawing lines you will make with pen and ink are similar to those I demonstrated earlier as pencil shading techniques.

Hatching

Is where parallel lines are used side by side in any, direction. The closer the lines are together, the darker the area; the further apart they are, the lighter the area.

Crosshatching

Is where the hatching lines are crossed over each other to achieve an effect.

Stippling

Is simply dots created with the tip of the pen. The more dots on an area, the darker it will become; the fewer dots, the lighter it will be.

Random Lines

Any type of line not covered in the other three groups. They could be tick-like marks suggesting tiles on a roof, or semicircles which could be used to create bushes and trees. On a piece of sketching paper practise the hatching, crosshatching, stippling and random lines. When you have tried these, experiment and see how many other types of pen mark and effects you can achieve. Also practice varying the pressure you apply to the nib, the heavier the pressure, the thicker the line; the gentler the pressure, the finer the line. Experiment by drawing everyday items in pen and ink around your home and garden. Draw the outline of the items lightly first with a pencil, then overdraw with pen and ink. Leave some items as a pen outline; the simplicity of this approach can be effective. Then try sketching similar items using hatching and crosshatching to create the textures and shading.

Pen and Ink Sketching

Use a kneaded eraser when the pen and ink sketch is dry to lift out any pencil guidelines. With practice you will soon discover just the right amount of hatching and crosshatching to use. Look for other examples of pen and ink sketches you may find around your home.

Look around the house and kitchen to find everyday objects to draw in pen and ink.

A salt mill

A. Sketch the object out in pencil.

B. Draw the outline in India ink with your pen.

A.　　B.　　C.

C. Using hatching, crosshatching, stippling and random lines, add the shading and textural effects.

A red pepper cut in half

Roadside Houses

I sketched this view in the delightful village of Churchtown on the outskirts of Southport.

Stage 1. Sketch the subject in light outline using a 2B pencil on sketching paper.

Stage 2. Lightly draw in the outline with pen and ink.

Roadside Houses

Stage 3. The light source is coming from the left, so the shadows are on the right of the objects in the sketch. The contrast between light and dark plays an important part in the success of the picture. Start using hatching and crosshatching to build up the shadows in each area. Use random lines to give the roof-tiles look, brickwork, foliage of the trees, texture of the foreground tree trunk, grass texture and windows in the way I show in the detail panel, below. Now go looking for more subjects of your own on which to practise this technique.

Tree trunk
Use hatching and crosshatching for the left hand tree trunk.

Bricks
Don't make them too neat, if old and weathered. Draw them using broken lines for some bricks.

Clouds. Use horizontal hatching behind the clouds to make them stand out

Then add an outline to the clouds.

Sketch roof

Add tiles.
Add diagonal hatching for tone . . . . . .

Add hatching for side of building in shade.

Candle

In the panel on page 26 showing types of pen marks I illustrated an area with stippling. Stippling is done using the tip of the pen to create dots. This can be a fascinating way of creating pictures. In this demonstration I show a candle in a candle stick holder. Try this out, and then see if you can find other subjects that would suit this technique.

Stage 1. Sketch the subject out lightly with your 2B pencil.

Stage 2. Using either your dip-in pen, or a medium or fine felt or nylon-tip pen, start from the top of the candle working your way down the picture stippling the whole subject. Use less dots in the lighter areas, increase them in the medium toned areas and add even more as each area, or part, becomes darker. Try to keep all the dots a similar size. Finally add the shadows of the background drape and tablecloth. Pastels, colored pencils, colored felt-tip pens, oil paint and acrylic paint can also be used for creating stippling paintings. The stippling technique was made very popular by the French artist, Georges Seurat.

Stage 2

Stage 1

Close up of stippling dots

Monochrome with Pen and Ink

The demonstration of the duck in the diagram to the side is an excellent way of recognizing and understanding the value of monochrome studies.

Stage 1. Make a tone strip like the one below by mixing small amounts of India ink with water on your pallet, adding more water to create the lighter tones and less for the darker tones.

Stage 2. Draw the outline of the duck using a 2B pencil
Tonal Test Strip

Stage 3. Brush the lightest tone on the duck as shown. Leave white paper for highlights, and let it dry.

Stage 4. Apply your medium tone as shown and let dry.

Stage 5. Apply your darkest tone last as shown and let dry.

Stage 6. Overdraw your pencil lines with pen and ink.

This demonstration helps you to understand about tone and the role it plays in sketching and painting. When you have tried the demonstration, look for subjects in color and try sketching them using this monochrome technique.

I often make monochrome studies, either for my own enjoyment, or as advanced preliminary sketches for major paintings. I have selected three monochrome sketches painted over the recent years from my portfolio. These are shown on the next page.

Monochromes

Top right. I saw my mother's steam iron on the kitchen table and found the monochrome technique helped me resolve the tricky problems in sketching this subject. I took an oblique view from above, looking down onto the iron. I used diluted India ink and then a felt-tipped pen to overdraw the pencil lines.

Bottom left. The Customs House, Kings Lynn. I made this monochrome sketch on location, and used it as a preliminary sketch towards making a finished painting of the subject. I used India ink and a dip-in pen to overdraw the pencil lines.

Bottom right. There are subjects all around us. I once simply opened the bathroom door, sat on the landing floor, which gave me a lower eyelevel, and sketched our bathroom sink in monochrome using diluted writing ink, and then overdrew it with a felt-tipped pen.

Iron

Customs House, Kings Lynn

Bathroom Sink

29

Cottage by the Sea

The previous demonstrations and advice provide a good foundation for all your future art work. Let me now introduce you to the joys of sketching with pen and wash in color. A pocket set of water colors, a No. 6 or No. 8 round water color brush, two glasses of water, a water color sketch pad, a 2B pencil, a kneaded eraser, together with your pen and ink, are all you need for this versatile technique.

Stage 1. Sketch out the subject with a 2B pencil.

Stage 2. Mix and apply a pale wash of color for each area. Let it dry.

Stage 3. Mix and apply a medium tone wash for each area, leaving parts of the lighter tones showing through.

Stage 4. Mix a darker wash and apply it as shown in the *Stage 3* picture. When dry, use a dip-in pen or a felt-tip pen and oversketch the picture. The resulting picture has a sharp, crisp look to it. Use this technique to produce quick sketches and finished art work.

Stage 1

Stage 2

Stage 3

Stage 4

Santorini

SANTORINI · GREECE·

Philip Beverill 1987.

Notre Dame

A water color or oil painting may take several hours to paint, but a pen and wash sketch can be completed in a fraction of the time. It is for this reason I often use this technique outdoors. When I am out with family or friends, or travelling, I often see splendid and appealing subjects, but due to the very limited time available it is not possible to paint a finished picture. Pen and wash with water color enables me to make a quick sketch, splash color onto it, and overdraw the essentials with my pen and ink. I then not only have a presentable and attractive sketch in its own right, but a sketch that provides material which can be developed into a finished painting in my studio. Let me show you several situations where I used the technique quickly to produce pictures which have a freshness or added quality that may have been lost by having unlimited time available to paint them.

I was tutoring on a cruise, sailing from Venice to Corfu, Dubrovnik, Santorini, through the Corinth Canal to Athens and on to Turkey. My task was to teach and demonstrate to the students on the cruise, not to go off painting my own pictures. But in free moments, coffee breaks and lunch breaks I would take out my pen and wash kit and sketch a view which caught my eye, like the breathtaking view in Santorini on the page opposite. The composition with the domed roof breaking the line of its distant hills was exciting and I only had fifteen minutes to capture the scene. I used water colors on sketching paper, overdrawing it with a fine felt-tip pen. Santorini, just for the price of a cup of coffee. Most people like to paint Notre Dame from the front. I was walking along the Left Bank in Paris, turned around and saw this rear view of Notre Dame. I knew I had to paint this view but it was soon going to rain. As a water color would have taken too long, I chose to do a pen and wash. The sketch took thirty minutes. Packing away my materials, the first rain drops started falling.

Venice

Gondolas are as much a part of Venice as are the pigeons in St. Mark's Square. The joy of the city is that it has not had to be adapted to accommodate automobiles. Venice is a marriage of sea and land. Venice is liquid light, a place where the sounds and sights which have captivated artists, musicians and authors over the past centuries have also cast its magic spell over me.

Below. Become an explorer. On one visit to Venice I decided to visit an area of the city unknown to me. I fortunately had my pen and wash kit with me when I came across the last gondola boatyard in Venice. The sketch below took forty-five minutes using a felt-tip pen over a water color sketch painted on 140lb paper.

I was intrigued by the single large tree in the center of the boatyard. This apparently has a design purpose; it is there to provide shade during the heat of the day for the boatyard workers. I was also intrigued to see the gondolas on their sides for repair... not quite the graceful upright position we see as they glide along the canals of the city.

Right. On another occasion I was teaching on one of my painting holiday courses in Venice. A particular view across the Grand Canal had often caught my eye and I felt it had the makings of a good subject. I liked the long, slender buildings and the Venetian lamppost. I discovered that if I sat on the pavement it would give me a low eyelevel and would have the effect of the lamppost appearing to intersect the line of the roofs. The top of the lamppost would be seen set against the sky. The lamppost also acted to link the foreground, the Grand Canal and the buildings on the other side of the canal. For speed I used pen and wash with water color to capture one of my favorite views on paper.

Pen and wash is addictive. Do not get hooked on it. The technique enables charming pictures to be produced so quickly that there is a temptation to draw black pen lines around every water color painting to finish the picture quickly. Don't let pen and wash studies be more than 25% of your picture production. This way you will retain the enjoyment of the technique to the overall benefit of your painting.

Gondola Boatyard, Venice.

View across the Grand Canal, Venice

Daffodil

How fortunate we are to be surrounded by so much natural beauty. Throughout the seasons we have an ever-changing wealth of flowers in our gardens, parks and floral shops. We grow them for our enjoyment and send cut flowers and potted plants as gifts to relatives and friends on special occasions. While floral painting deserves a whole book to itself, you can start to sketch flowers from the very first day you pick up a pencil and paper. I have shown several sketches which you may like to try. They are an excellent way to start floral subjects.

Daffodil.

This was a single bloom with leaves from our garden, cut and placed in a tall, thin, clear, glass vase of water. The vase had a heavy base. I allowed the flower to curve slightly to the right, rather than have everything too straight. Choose a similar subject from your garden or use this study. Sketch the subject out with a 2B pencil. Using water colors tint the flower, stem and leaves of the flower, leaving the vase in pencil. The idea of using just a splash of color in a sketch, to focus attention on the main feature, can give a distinctive look.

Rose.

At first, choose flowers with distinctive petals and leaves, do not paint very small flowers. The rose is perhaps one of the most beautiful of flowers. I bought this single rose for my daughter but could not resist sketching it. From one rose you can produce four different types of sketch and learn so much about each technique and the

structure of the flower. The top left study shows the rose just in pencil outline. The top right study is a pencil sketch with the addition of shading. The bottom left study is a water color sketch. Finally try the sketch in water color overdrawn with pen and ink. One subject, four different treatments. If you try four studies of a different flower each month, you will soon gain expertise in sketching and painting flowers.

A Rose

Pencil outline

Pencil with shading

Color Notes

As we are now using water colors as an important part of adding color to our sketches, you will find it helpful to make out the color chart on the right. While most water color boxes have a good selection of colors in them, many colors can be made by mixing just three *Primary Colors*, Red, Yellow and Blue. By mixing any two of the three primary colors, you make the Secondary Colors. Red and Yellow make Orange, Yellow and Blue make Green, Blue and Red make Mauve. If you mix any two of the secondary colors, you make the *Tertiary Colors*. Orange and Mauve make Dark Brown, Orange and Green make Light Brown, and Mauve and Green make Olive Green. By mixing the three *Primary Colors*, Red, Yellow and Blue, with very little water you can make Black. Brown and Blue mixed together will make Grey.

The water color sketch shown below is of items that were lying on our kitchen table one morning, an eggcup, a spoon and a knife. This sketch was painted using colors made by mixing the primary colors.

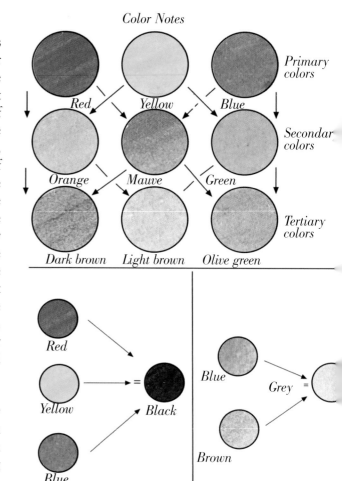

Color Notes

Red Yellow Blue — Primary colors

Orange Mauve Green — Secondary colors

Dark brown Light brown Olive green — Tertiary colors

Red + Yellow + Blue = Black

Blue + Brown = Grey

Pinocchio

It is important to learn how different mediums can impart their own distinct look to a subject. In this demonstration I used Pinocchio, a wooden doll I once bought for my daughter. He is a cheerful fellow and very colorful.

This demonstration can be applied to almost any subject. Using a 2B pencil, sketch the subject out. Use a ruler to divide it into five sections. Sketch or color in each section with a different medium. I used water color, pen and wash, colored pencil, pen and ink and a graphite pencil. You may be quite surprised at the visual differences between the mediums and feel that if you were going to sketch or paint the whole subject in one medium you might choose colored pencil, while another artist may feel he or she would like to render the subject in water color. This puts you in control of your sketch. Not only can you choose a subject that appeals to you, but you can choose the medium you feel the subject would look best in. Sensing the right medium for a subject is very much part of the skill of being an artist.

Water color →

Pen and wash →

Colored pencil →

Pencil →   Pen and ink →

Composition

There are certain guidelines that if followed, can help you build your work on sound compositional foundations. One of the most important things to avoid is having any line or object that cuts your picture into two equal halves. Set any such line or object to one side or other.

Focal points and key lines

Decide what it is that you want the viewer to look at. Ensure their eyes will not wander, as if the viewer is lost. You are the artist, you are in control, be decisive.

A picture should have a focal point, that is, a main feature to which the eye may draw. I show three views. In the first, the focal point, the cottage, is in the middle distance. In the second the focal point, the ship, is in the far distance. In the third the fisherman in the foreground is the focal point.

A picture should also have key lines of the composition leading the eyes of the viewer to the focal point. I have arrowed the key lines of the three compositions and I think from these illustrations you will see how the use of the focal point and key lines help bring a composition together.

Halfway

Halfway

Halfway

Halfway

Composition

The Triangle

Often a triangle can offer an excellent shape on which to base a composition, especially a still life or floral study. I have a still life made up from a group of toys. I have placed the teddy bear to the right so the apex of the triangle is off-centre. The rose in the vase forms the upright of the triangle, with the handbag and powder compact forming the base. The tree creates the triangle's upright side, with the landscape and church forming the bottom and third, sloping side, of the triangle. Try to ensure that still life and floral studies have height, width, and depth to them. If you now go and look at paintings, or prints of paintings, by any of the great masters, or by any fine artist, you will almost certainly find that their most successful paintings employ many of the important compositional points that I have referred to here.

Perspective

Perspective is the one area of drawing and painting in which most people experience some degree of difficulty. When most people hear perspective mentioned they go to a bookshop or a library, obtain a book on the subject, flip through it, see lines shooting about all over, and usually end up more confused than before. The secret is to keep the whole business of perspective as simple as possible, to remember a few basic rules, and to bear in mind that perspective is not something one masters all in one, two, or three lessons. Learning about perspective is an on-going learning process. One goes along over a period of months, indeed years, collecting together the pieces of information, like pieces of a jigsaw, until they all fit together and the picture, the theory of perspective, becomes clear and easy to apply to one's work. Most men used to have an advantage over women when taking up drawing and painting, because at school most learned basic carpentry, and even some metalwork. Some boys learned basic technical drawing and on leaving school and entering working life read books, manuals, and journals filled with line- drawings, plans, front elevations, and side elevations of all sorts of subjects. This basic familiarity with line is very handy when learning to paint.

fig. 1

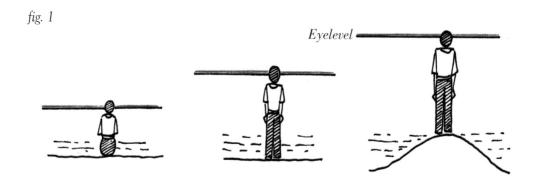

Eyelevel

Perspective

The eyelevel is an imaginary line, horizontally across your field of vision when you look straight ahead, not up, nor down, but straight ahead. In my sketch, I show a figure sitting low down, as if on a beach, then standing, then standing on a sand dune (*fig. 1*). Note how the eyelevel is always directly ahead of the figure. When looking at a real subject look straight ahead, hold a ruler straight out with the thin edge in front of, and across your eyes, and that is where your eyelevel is. Which comes first, the drawing in of the eyelevel or the object? Generally I suggest you draw in the object lightly first, then apply the eyelevel and use it with the rules of perspective to check and correct the object. One way to see perspective in action is to picture the view looking along railway lines. They appear to merge in the distance. They appear to become smaller and closer together. The point where they appear to merge is known as the Vanishing Point. We know they do not merge in reality. I show this in my sketch (*fig. 2*). I also show the railway lines with telegraph poles on the left, then with three trees on the right. The telegraph poles and the trees in a drawing or painting would also appear to become smaller and closer together as they recede. I have shown the guidelines for each item, illustrating how the guidelines meet at the vanishing point

fig. 2

Vanishing point

VP

Perspective

Next I show a front view of a tool box. With this view there is just one vanishing point on the horizon line for the sides of the box. I am imagining that I am sitting on a chair at a table, drawing the box in front of me. If I look straight ahead, over the box, my horizon line would be about 12" (30.5cm) above the top of the tool box. In my next sketch the box is set at an angle. We now have two vanishing points, one for each side. Guidelines will often want to converge at vanishing points off the page. This is quite normal and often happens. When it does, lay scrap paper at the side and tape it on from behind, then extend the guidelines onto it, in the way I show in my sketch. Never guess or assume the perspective is correct, always try to prove it.

Vanishing point

fig. 3

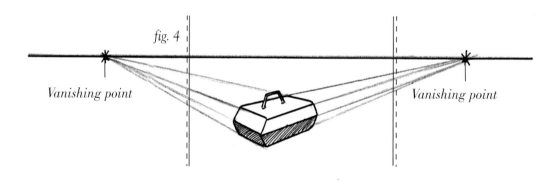

fig. 4

Vanishing point   *Vanishing point*

Circular Perspective

Few people realize that perspective helps to solve the problems of drawing circles and ellipses, but it can. I have illustrated this in a sketch of three saucepans with one on its side (*fig. 5*). I have lightly drawn the group out and have placed my eyelevel well above it. I have then drawn a light guiding square around each ellipse we can see and have drawn those squares 'in perspective', in the same way as the television. The squares for the ellipses each have their respective vanishing points on the common eyelevel. The two upright pans share the same vanishing point as their ellipses are on the same plane. The ellipses for the pan on its side are on a different plane so have their own vanishing point at a different position on the eyelevel. The use of the squares helps determine where each vanishing point should be, to ensure the true perspective of the subject where there is an ellipse involved. I then go back to each ellipse and check it touches the centre of each side of the square it occupies, for provided it does, I know the ellipse must be in perspective. Gently rub out the squares used outside of each ellipse and perspective guidelines before a picture is shaded in or painted.

fig. 5

Vanishing point

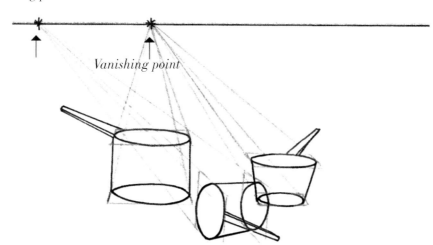

Vanishing point

44

Heads, Portraits, Figures

This demonstration is intended as a quick guide. Drawing faces is a subject that deserves an entire book, however, there are a few basic rules that if followed correctly should help you to sketch faces successfully

Sketch A. Rule 1 is that the head is an Egg Shape

Sketch B. The second rule is use *Halfway lines.* The center of the eyes are on a line halfway between the top of the skull and bottom of the chin. The bottom of the nose is on a line halfway between the center of the eye line and the bottom of the chin. The middle of the mouth is on a line halfway between the bottom of the nose and the chin. The top of the ears are just above the line for the center of the eyes. The bottom of the ears are on the bottom of the nose line.

Sketch C. A vertical line down the center of the face sees the eyes, nose, mouth and ears divided equally either side of it.

Sketch D. I have turned those halfway guidelines into ellipses and placed the features on them. This starts to bring the face into circular perspective and helps with any foreshortening of the face. We can now use head D and start to maneuver it to overcome all sorts of positional problems. Simply turn the egg and guidelines to the left, E, and to the right, F. Point the center of the egg to the left or right and tilt it back, G. We can alter the incline of the head. To give the head backward look, H, place the curves steeper on the egg, or to give the downward look dip the curves downward. This helps achieve the foreshortening of the features and head. The contours of the face, hair and features can be built up on the foundation of the egg shape and guidelines of any face. Copy these sketches and then practise using photographs of faces and real faces.

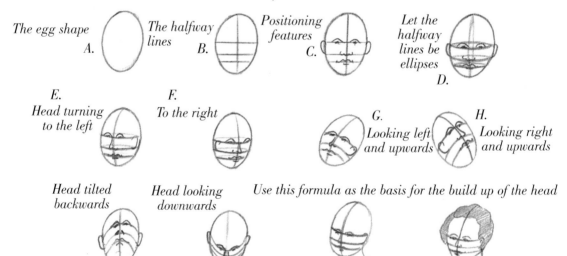

The egg shape — A.

The halfway lines — B.

Positioning features — C.

Let the halfway lines be ellipses — D.

E. Head turning to the left

F. To the right

G. Looking left and upwards

H. Looking right and upwards

Head tilted backwards

Head looking downwards

Use this formula as the basis for the build up of the head

Heads, Portraits, Figures

Practise sketching features from photographs and from life. Look in a mirror and sketch your own features. Look at an eye and pay close attention to detail. Note the tear duct in the corner near the nose, highlight on the black pupil of the eye, tone of the iris, the way the eyelids clip the top and bottom of the iris. Note the shading on the white of the eye and the shading in the folds of flesh above and below the eyelids. Note the shading under the lobes of the nose and nostril, and the shadow on the top lip.

When the mouth is closed the top lip is very dark. The lower lip has shading, but also highlights. Show the fine lines curving over the lower lip. When the mouth is open hint at the teeth and make the cavity in the mouth very dark. Avoid severe outlines.

The eyes, nose and mouth are dominant features. The ears are a secondary feature. Understate the ears; do not make them as clearly defined as the other features unless it is unavoidable.

Some common mistakes   *The correct way*

Eyes

Noses

Mouth (Closed)

(Open)

Ears

Heads, Portraits, Figures

Learning the proportions and developing a practical technique are the keys to sketching figures successfully. There are 8 heads in the length of the male figure, 7½ heads in the length of the female figure and 4½ heads in the young child figure. Copy the proportion sketch on the right to imprint these proportions on your mind. There are three types of figure in a sketch or painting, the far distance figure, the middle distance figure and the foreground figure. Let us look at proportions and techniques for sketching the middle distance figure as this is the type most often seen in general landscape sketches and paintings. The technique can be applied to all other figures.

I show how to use stick figures to position the figure. I add a chest and pelvis, locate the shoulder, elbow, knee joints, hands and feet. I usually sketch these very lightly in pencil and then sketch the actual figure and clothes on that foundation. The same technique can be used for standing, sitting, static or moving figures. Try pencil and pen and ink sketches of these types of figures. Do not put in too much detail. Keep them simple.

Figures

Proportions of a man, woman and child in relation to each other

Static figure

Stage 1 Stage 2 Stage 3

Moving figure

Stage 1 Stage 2 Stage 3

Seated figure

Standing figure

Portrait on a Train

Practise sketching features from photographs and from life. Look in a mirror and sketch your own features. Look at an eye and pay close attention to detail. Note the tear duct in the corner near the nose, the highlight on the black pupil of the eye, the tone of the iris, the way the eyelids clip the top and bottom of the iris. Note the shading on the white of the eye and the shading in the folds of flesh above and below the eyelids. Note the shading under the lobes of the nose and nostril, and the shadow on the top lip. When the mouth is closed the top lip is very dark. The lower lip has shading, but also highlights. Show the fine lines curving over the lower lip. When the mouth is open hint at the teeth and make the cavity in the mouth very dark. Avoid severe outlines. The eyes, nose and mouth are dominant features. The ears are a secondary feature. Understate the ears; do not make them as clearly defined as the other features unless it is unavoidable. This character was sitting just a few yards from me on a train one day. Using water colors oversketched with a felt-tip pen, I found the above figure drawing technique worked equally well for this closer figure.

Sketching Outdoors

Many people are apprehensive at first about sketching outdoors. There is no need to be. You can simply look out of your window and draw the view you see, or go into your back garden or a friend's garden and sketch a corner of it. There is nothing quite like sketching and painting outdoors. You become very much part of the scene which you are painting. When painting from a photograph everything you see has been frozen for a split second, but compare that to being outdoor, you can feel the warmth of the sun, the gentle breeze, the sky is active, the clouds move, the light changes, any water flows, you can hear the sounds of people, birds or other features which may be part of your subject.

A viewfinder is a window 3" x 2¼" (75mm x 55mm) cut out of a piece of card 9" x 6¼" (230 mm x 160mm). Held at arm's length this can be used to frame various areas of an outdoor view to help you decide what, and how much of the view, you want in your picture. Hold it horizontally, then see if you can find upright views by holding the viewfinder so the rectangle in the center is vertical.

Keep the subjects simple and not too cluttered. If you encounter a subject with tricky perspective like the rowing boat shown on the page opposite, When sketching outdoors keep the kit light and simple. A sketch pad, 2B pencil, pencil sharpener, putty eraser, pocket set of water colors, a No. 6 or No. 8 round brush, small bottle of water, two small containers to pour the water into, some tissues to clean your brush and a fine felt-tip pen are all you need for many happy hours of outdoor sketching.

Peel Harbour, Isle of Man

Sketching Outdoors

Viewfinder

View

Using viewfinder to select subject area

Pencil and wash sketch of selected area

Using a box as the basis
for drawing a rowing boat

Sketching and Painting from Photographs

Some artist say never copy, only work from life. Others say copying is perfectly acceptable. My feeling is that a camera and photographs can be a great aid to the artist, providing that he or she does not become a slave to them. As a source of back up reference material they have many uses. You can of course learn to paint sunsets, snow, seascapes, animals, foreign views and many other subjects from photographs, perhaps when there is no possibility of doing so from life. A quick outdoor sketch, supported by a photograph you took of the subject, can also provide all the material you need for a future painting at home. Animals, birds and subjects which move too quickly for you to sketch, can be sketched and painted from photographs. The secret is to try to bring the subject to life. This can be achieved with a little imagination, by thinking yourself into the view, or in front of the animal, bird or subject. I was on the Isle of Man when I came across this delightful Manx cottage. To obtain the best view meant going into the owners garden, and in such circumstances an artist must ask the owners permission to sketch or to take a photograph. Usually, as on this occasion, the owner is only too pleased to let you take a photograph and make a sketch. As it was late afternoon I did not have the time to paint the cottage. The daylight would soon be lost. The combination of photograph and sketch meant I would be able to work from these to produce a finished painting in my studio.

A Manx Cottage.

Sketching and Painting from Photographs

Fountains Abbey. This was a photograph one of my students took. It was a little dark, but had possibilities. I decided that if he made a circular painting, based on the center, it would make an interesting picture. The trees on the left and right were not essential to the painting. This was very much a situation of finding a picture within a picture. I illustrated the idea to him in a sketch.

Stage 1.

The photograph of Fountains Abbey. A good possible subject in the center, too dark at the sides.

Stage 2.

I cut a circle out of a piece of card to frame the area of interest in the photograph.

Stage 3.

I used pen and wash to sketch out the Abbey, the immediate lansdcape and figures. I modified the trees on the left and decided this would provide a good subject for a painting.

Stage 2.

Stage 1.

Stage 3.

Sketches for a Mural

Sketches produced on one occasion can sometimes be used on another occasion. I was asked by clients if I would paint a mural for their new, indoor swimming pool. The subject they had in mind was northern Italy and the Italian lakes. I had a folder full of recent sketches of the area, except for the Italian lakes. For the far end wall I combined two sketches, one of Villa Pitiana, a 12th century palace set against the Tuscan hills, the other, a view of a farm at the foot of the Tuscan hills. Although I had not visited the lakes so had no sketches, I decided to use a selection of photographs to compose the subject for the left-hand wall. The whole mural was designed to look as if it were one view.

The two photographs on the right show the finished mural painted in acrylic paint. The sketch immediately below was to show the client how the mural would look in their swimming pool.

Colored Pencils

Colored pencils provide a convenient way to add color to a sketch. They can be used in a variety of different ways. There are two types of colored pencil, water soluble and non-water soluble. They can be bought in sets or individually. They can be used dry on sketching paper, or wet on a smooth 90lb, or 140lb, water color paper. Try using them dry first. Lightly draw out a subject and then color and shade it with the colored pencils. As with normal graphite pencils you can increase or decrease the tonal strength by varying the pressure you apply. You can also superimpose one color on another to achieve fascinating color variations. I show two sketches using water soluble colored pencils dry. One is of a farm on a hill, the other is a coastal view looking out to sea. The left half of the farm landscape uses dry colored pencils. On the right half of the farm sketch I have shown how brushing a little water over the colored pencil imparts a water color look to it. When dry, the picture can be oversketched again using the dry technique where appropriate. The view looking out to sea uses dry colored pencils.

Pastels

Pastels are a mixture of pigment, chalk and pipe clay. They vary from very soft to firm and come in round or square sticks. The artist normally snaps the stick into pieces of different lengths and then sketches and works with the tips, sides and edges of the pastel, applying the dry color directly to the paper. The most common pastel paper is known as Ingres paper. It comes in a range of colors, from light to very dark, and has a slightly coarse texture which enables the pastel to grip the surface. Pastel sketching is when the artist uses the pastel directly on the paper and lets the color of the paper become an integral part of the picture in the way I have done with my vegetable sketch. One color of pastel can be overlaid on another. Pastel painting is when the finger is used to gently smudge and blend the pastel to achieve often delightful effects. The background paper is fully covered, so the color of the paper is less important.

It is also possible to buy pastel pencils. These are encased in wood and the artist works with the point to give a more detailed appearance to the picture. Many artists build up a collection of each type of pastel. Pastel pictures are normally 'fixed' with a light spray of clear fixative to minimise the risk of the pastel smudging accidentally.

A pad, or sheet, of pastel paper, a box of 12 assorted pastels including a white and a black, a can of aerosol fixative, a kneaded eraser and a stiff dry paintbrush are all you need to start pastel sketching. The dry brush is used to jab at any errors to loosen the pastel, which you then gently blow away before rubbing the area with the eraser.

Keep a damp cloth in a plastic bag by you so you can take the cloth out to wipe your fingers when working with pastels. This keeps your fingers clean and the bag keeps the cloth damp

Pastels

Pastel sketch. Vegetables

Pastel painting. Landscape

Oil Painting

Many artists paint with oil paints but do not realise you can use them for sketching. As oil paints normally require several days to become touch dry, many people think they are not a practical medium for sketching. I can tell you of two very successful ways to use them for this purpose.

Tinted Canvas Panel.

If sketching outdoors, take a canvas panel, your oil paints and materials with you, making sure you have some clean turpentine. When you find a subject that appeals to you, sketch it out lightly with a 2B pencil on the canvas panel. Then, mix your oil paints colors with small amounts of turpentine to create a thin consistency. Tint the various colored areas of your canvas with the thinned paint. Within 30 to 60 minutes the turpentine will have evaporated and the panel will be dry. You can then take this panel, and others you may tint, home. On cold, wet, winter days, or dark evenings, take a panel out and paint the fully finished oil painting on top of your original, tinted oil color panel.

The same technique can be used indoors, but lends itself well to outside painting expeditions and holidays.

Liquin.

The other method is to use Liquin, an alkyd resin produced by Winsor and Newton, that you can mix with your oil paints instead of turpentine or linseed oil for normal oil painting techniques. It accelerates the drying of the oil paint. I use it frequently, and find if I am on holiday and mix Liquin with my oil paint to paint the oil paintings at the beginning of the holiday, the pictures are touch dry at the end of the holiday and can, with care, be transported home safely. Alkyd paints are synthetic paints similar to oils, but based in Liquin. They are normally touch dry within 18 hours. Wear old clothes when working with oil paints. Oils are lovely to use, but dabs of color can get on to your clothes, no matter how careful you are.

Subject. Lakeland bridge

Subject drawn out on a canvas panel

Oil Painting

Partially tinted Oil Panel Sketch

Finished tinted Oil Panel Sketch

Lord Street, Southport

Inspiration and imagination do not come in tubes or bottles. For twelve years I owned an art store and framed pictures. One day a lady asked to have a picture framed. Her husband was a keen fisherman and had been salmon fishing in Scotland. While there he bought a long, thin, pencil sketch of the salmon river with inset sketches of the salmon pools along each side. It was a charming idea and the long, thin shape attracted me. Southport does not have a salmon river, but it has a very famous street over a mile long, called Lord Street. It is very straight and a central feature of the town with many historic buildings, shops and hotels situated either side of it. I thought

Lord Street, Southport

I could adapt the salmon river idea to the street featuring key buildings and the town's history instead of salmon pools. I selected the most interesting buildings, made sketches of them, and used pen and ink to draw out the finished art work in my studio. I had it screen printed and then sold it framed and unframed, in black and white and hand water colored versions. Measuring 9¼" x 36"(235mm x 910mm) it has proven to be very popular with residents and visitors to the town. Southport's local authority commissioned 200 framed, slightly different versions of the print, to be the town's gift, presented by the Mayors of Southport to very important visitors. Can you adapt a familiar location in an imaginative way?

Framing Sketches

Keep loose sketches clean and flat in a portfolio. There will be sketches that you decide to frame and exhibit or sell. Some people make their own frames, but the majority of people call on the help of a professional picture framer, or buy and use many of the very good, ready-made frames and mats which can often be found in art and framing stores. Some framers advertise a mail order service in art catalogues.

Pencil, colored pencils, pen and ink, water color and pastel sketches will need to be framed with a mat of a suitable color and under glass. The glass protects the picture from atmospheric soiling. The mat provides a border between the surrounding wall and the sketch and keeps the glass away from the immediate picture surface.

Oil paint sketches, which are not too thickly painted, can be framed the same way, but generally, and especially if thickly or robustly painted, oil paintings are varnished and framed without glass.

A good framer can be a very good friend, offering expert advice on what will show your sketches and paintings to the best advantage.

Exhibiting and Selling your Work.

Most people like to keep their first pictures, or give them to family or friends. As the standard of your work develops, start to consider the opportunities to exhibit and sell some of that work. I would certainly recommend considering joining a local arts club or society. Art galleries and libraries usually have details for such groups. You will often find helpful support, friendship, visiting artists demonstrating their techniques, and the opportunity to show work will all become available to you. Galleries and libraries usually have details of forthcoming local, regional, and national exhibitions. Exhibitions can vary from pictures hung on walls on street railings, to seeing work on the walls of a famous gallery. Local stores, restaurants, and building societies often take and display art on a sale or return basis. It is customary to offer a percentage of such a sale to that establishment. Most towns and cities have open exhibitions where artists in the vicinity submit work. As more work often enters than there is space to hang, a selection committee often chooses work. Acceptance is an exhilarating feeling. Many people find rejection dispiriting. Good work often finds rejection due to the lack of space. It may be that they already have similar painting. Work rejected by one exhibit often finds acceptance at another.

You can always mark your painting NFS or Not for Sale, if you want to display, but do not want to sell them. If you offer work for sale but find yourself uncertain the price to charge a local framer or a senior member of an art gallery have knowledge of current prices.

Keep copies of the receipts for art materials and frames that you buy, and any expense you incur, and the sales that you make, in case you find you income from such sales as taxable. Copyright is the infringement of an artist's exclusive right to determine the copy of their work. It holds for the period of seventy to one hundred years after the artist's death. Many artists, especially art tutors and artist/authors like me have no objection to student copying paintings as a means to learning the art of painting.